PTSD WORKBOOK
FOR TEEN GIRLS

A Fun Guide to Heal Trauma and Dealing with Emotions

Nightmares and Vivid Flashbacks

By

Delores R.

Sellix Publications

ABOUT THE AUTHOR

Delores R. Introducing the incredible author behind the empowering "PTSD Workbook for Teen Girls," Delores R. Embarking on a remarkable journey of healing and resilience, Delores brings a wealth of knowledge and personal experience to this transformative guide. Delores is not just an author but also a passionate advocate for mental health and well-being. Drawing from her own battles with trauma and the triumphs she encountered along the way, Delores has become a beacon of hope for teen girls navigating the challenges of PTSD.

Her unique perspective and compassionate approach make this workbook an invaluable resource for anyone seeking to heal from trauma and overcome the distressing symptoms of PTSD. Delores understands first-hand the impact that nightmares and vivid flashbacks can have on a young girl's life, and she is dedicated to providing effective tools and strategies to manage and conquer these difficult emotions.

Through her expertise and commitment, Delores has created a safe space within the pages of this workbook, guiding teen girls with warmth and empathy. Her profound understanding of the complexities of PTSD allows her to connect deeply with readers, empowering them to take charge of their healing journey and embrace a future filled with strength, resilience, and joy. As you embark on this transformative experience, allow Delores R. to be your trusted companion, guiding you step by step towards healing, emotional well-being, and reclaiming your power. With her unwavering support and wealth of knowledge, Delores invites you to embark on a journey of self-discovery and transformation, helping you find solace, growth, and the freedom to live a life of strength and purpose.

Join Delores R. on this remarkable journey and discover the incredible power within you to heal, thrive, and rewrite your story. Together, let's embrace a future filled with hope, resilience, and endless possibilities.

CONTENTS

INTRODUCTION

On a very fine morning, you may wake up to a dazzling morning sunbeam with a warm breeze through your window. It is as pleasant as sparking a wave of euphoria through your whole body. But! As soon as you get in touch with the world around you, a few hours later, nothing seems to be the same. It may be because of a phone call in which someone conversed with you about a tragedy. It may be a news report regarding a car accident, reminiscing about the incident involving a car accident that

has killed your loved one. Maybe an earthquake or a tornado that swoops down and shatters everything. Then, there you are, standing on a precipice with a bag of pebbles burdening you with each passing day. *What do you plan to do? Do you plan to quit, stand there with the bag, die, hide, leave the bag there, and go on?* After winning a huge battle inside you, you may believe that the world around you is generous and meaningful; everything that happens or will happen will be part of your life story. You may assume that you were worthy of good and pleasant things that could happen to you. You may start to feel secure and lovable in this world. Unfortunately, you are struck with trauma, and it seems you are losing control over what is happening around you. You feel vulnerable, unsafe, and insecure; the meaning of a worthy life appears to dwindle.

There are a few general, basic assumptions to guide one's life before the traumatic event. What is trauma? *What does it mean to work through it, survive it, or get over it?* The first step towards healing is to recognize its impact. A traumatic event can have various associated effects, disturbing your feelings, emotions, thoughts, relationships, manners, outlooks, and hopefulness. Yet, it can give you a new direction toward a purposeful life.

Humans are not Robots

"There is a void between a stimulus and its response, and that void holds the power to choose a response where our growth and freedom lie."

Victor Frankl (Jewish-Austrian psychiatrist)

Victor Frankl is well known for his work in logotherapy, where he describes a man's search for life's meaning and goodness to help others as a central human motivational force. His study implies how humans often react in certain situations. Mostly, we do not choose our behaviours as much and act situationally. He observed that void before a reaction came. He suggested we could learn, grow, and change by recognizing and utilizing this void. With this awareness, we can find peace and happiness in the internal and external pressures that control our reactions.

Humans are not robots; they experience complex ideas, feelings, and emotions. Since it makes us human, responding to traumatic circumstances is very normal. Most of us begin life as kind, trustworthy individuals. Trauma challenges some of our fundamental presumptions about the world. *For instance, many people believe that bad things do not happen to nice people or that the world is predictable.* Trauma is challenging to process independently since it modifies your fundamental worldview.

PART ONE: SELF-DISCOVERY OF PTSD

CHAPTER 1: TRAUMA; A DISTRESSING EMOTIONAL RESPONSE

1.1 Understanding Trauma

Trauma is a profound psychological and emotional reaction that occurs in response to a traumatic incident or experience, significantly impacting a person's ability to cope. Various situations, such as physical or sexual assault, natural disasters, accidents, war or terrorism, and emotional abuse or neglect, can lead to trauma.

In everyday language, people sometimes use the terms "traumatic" and "stressful" interchangeably. However, it's important to recognize that trauma and stress are distinct. Those who have experienced trauma can attest to this. While daily inconveniences like a long commute or chronic challenges such as unemployment can be unpleasant, traumatic experiences pose a genuine risk to life. When it comes to a tragic event:

✓ *You are directly involved in or witness an event that presents a real threat of death or severe injury.*

✓ *You encounter or witness a situation in which your own or someone else's physical safety is in grave danger.*

✓ *You experience intense fear, helplessness, or terror as a result of what you have seen or experienced.*

From this list, it becomes evident why events like combat, physical or sexual assault, natural disasters, or car accidents are considered traumatic. They involve a significant risk to both physical safety and life, either for oneself or others in the vicinity. In Activity 1, you will explore potentially distressing life events. Keep in mind that an unidentified traumatic event (or events) must meet the criteria of posing a severe physical threat to life and safety, whether it's yours or someone else's. The purpose of this exercise is not to overwhelm you. You simply need to reflect on whether any of these experiences have occurred in your life; there's no need to delve deeply into them. Taking the first step toward healing involves acknowledging these events, which requires courage.

Activity 1: What Have You Gone Through?

This activity has been designed to determine if you have ever gone through anything horrific and, if so, what it was. Write down whether you encountered or observed any type of traumatic event or events and, if yes, whether it put your life, another person's life, or both at risk. Briefly, (in a few words or a sentence) describe your response to the incident.

Traumatic Event:_____

_____

_____

_____

_____

_____

Did I experience it myself or witnessed it with someone else?

_____

_____

_____

_____

_____

Whose life was in danger or whose safety was threatened?

_____

_____

_____

_____

_____

My Reaction

_____

_____

_____

_____

1.2 Trauma-associated Reactions

What transpires after a traumatic event or sequence of events? There are numerous possible responses you could have. You can initially experience shock, anxiety, or a sense that what happened was weird or unbelievable. Dissociation is a phenomenon where you experience numbness and the sensation of leaving your body. You might not even be able to recall any or all of the specifics of what just took place. Your responses might alter if you have experienced horrific occurrences that seem to last lifetime. You can feel as though you have spent your entire life in a battle zone; you are constantly on guard and prepared to attack at any time. You might not even be aware of your identity. People respond differently to traumatic, frightening, and risky events than to other situations. Three responses to terrible events are always possible: *fight, run, or freeze.* These responses happen spontaneously and are controlled by a fundamental part of your brain. There is no opportunity for you to choose your response.

The reflexive employment of overly adaptive coping strategies in the actual or perceived presence of a traumatic event is referred to as a trauma reaction. The four most widely recognised trauma responses are *fight, flight, freeze, and fawn,* also referred to as the "4 Fs of trauma."

Trauma-Associated Reactions

Fight: Threat confrontation.

Flight: Hide from the threat.

Freeze: Shut down threat response.

Fawn: Soothe with the threat.

Fight

"The fight response, when utilised in response to trauma can be helpful in creating boundaries and asserting oneself, can become negative and lead to anger and aggression. This behaviour is motivated by fear and a desire to reclaim control by addressing the threat." *A fight trauma reaction occurs when one believes they can regain control of the situation by exerting dominance over the perceived* threat. This can manifest in various ways, including engaging in physical altercations, yelling or screaming, displaying aggressive behavior, throwing objects, or causing damage to property. Additionally, it may be expressed through physical symptoms such as clenching the jaw, crying uncontrollably, experiencing stomach discomfort, or tightly gripping the hands into fists.

Flight

The flight reaction is associated with avoidant behavior in challenging situations. When in a state of good health, it is normal to disengage to a certain extent when faced with unpleasant conditions. However, as a trauma response, the flight reaction takes avoidance to an extreme level, resulting in complete isolation.

The flight response occurs when individuals believe that they can avoid harm by removing themselves from the danger, thereby preventing a confrontation. This may manifest as a strong inclination to flee and avoid social contact altogether. It can involve actively seeking ways to escape uncomfortable situations or withdrawing from interactions when things become challenging. In order to cope with distressing circumstances, individuals may choose to keep themselves occupied or run away from difficult situations. This flight response serves as a way to protect oneself from perceived threats and maintain a sense of safety.

Freeze

When acting normally, the freeze reaction might assist you in slowing down and carefully evaluating the circumstance to decide what to do next. *The freeze response is connected to immobilising behaviors and dissociation when it's harmful. When this defence is used, it frequently has the effect of "freezing" a person physically, rendering them immobile, or causing them to become disoriented or disengaged from reality.* You don't feel like you're truly there, and you're cognitively disoriented as you try to find emotional safety by ignoring what's going on around you and how you're feeling. It is the same as momentary paralysis and disengaging from your body to reduce stress.

Fawn

Fawning is fundamentally about appeasing others and exhibiting pacifying behaviours. It is distinguished by putting others first and doing everything it takes to avoid confrontation and win their approval. To ensure safety, it may appear beneficial to be loved and to show deference to others, but this is not the case if you lose sight of who you are. By completely blending with others, it could get to the point where you give up on yourself and your wants. Most likely, you feel unnoticed by others and possibly that others in your life have overtaken you. The fawn response is so people-pleasing that it causes you to completely forget about your thoughts, feelings, and physical experiences.

Activity 2: Write About Your Trauma and Your Reactions Associated with it!

Rose was so terrified when she smelled smoke and heard the fire alarm in her home that she fled out and down the street. Until she reached the end of her street, she ran without even realising it. She came closer to the house to look for the rest of her family after waiting for the fire brigade to arrive.

Brida's football coach sexually assaulted her. She froze when the coach first touched her inappropriately, unable to move or speak. Now she regrets not resisting the coach's advances and for not resolutely yelling, "No!" Brida feels reluctant to discuss what occurred to her because she didn't protest or object. She fears that people will assume that she approved of the inappropriate contact.

Accidentally hurt in an automobile; Jacob. In the initial moments following the collision, he tried to fight the paramedics and keep everyone away from him. Later, after realising that they are there to assist him, he consented to their transport to the hospital. Once he arrived at the hospital, he found it difficult to comprehend why he would fight with those who were attempting to assist him.

Joey feels the nagging urge to start wanting to be like them, to please them, to keep trying, to keep shaping himself into what he thinks they want instead of admitting that they are abusive or just don't like him when he is rejected by me?" he asks himself in precise terms. "Is it because of x, y, or z? Will you just accept me if I do this?"

How would you convince Jacob that his reaction is both expected and normal?

_____

_____

_____

_____

If Rose did not know what she was doing at the time, how would you explain to her that her response made sense?

_____

_____

_____

_____

What would you say to Brida to let her know that you recognise his desire for the contact to occur?

_____

_____

_____

_____

What would you suggest to Joey to maintain boundaries and accept himself as he is?

_____

_____

_____

_____

Which responses you made were intense, hazardous, or traumatising circumstances?

_____

_____

_____

_____

Write the type of reaction (fight, escape, or freeze) before each reaction as you describe it in the lines below.

Reation:_____

Reaction: _____

Reaction: _____

Can you now describe any of your earlier fight, flight, or freeze responses that you were not aware of at the time? In that case, please describe them here:

_____
_____
_____
_____

1.3 Trauma and Your Beliefs

Beliefs are "knowings" or things you instinctively feel are true or think are true. Your beliefs and perceptions about yourself, other people, and the world may have an impact on your behaviors and decisions. The exercise that follows covers several beliefs that could develop as a result of being exposed to trying circumstances. Traumatic situations can cause your perceptions about your five fundamental psychological needs—needs for protection, trust, power, esteem, and intimacy—to change. Recognising the impact of trauma on your life and learning what beliefs can be challenged or adjusted is one way to ascertain the impact of trauma on your life.

Activity 3: You and Your Trauma Associated Beliefs

Write about a scenario or circumstances in which a belief developed or influenced your actions or decisions. Examine the beliefs that apply to you. When discussing these circumstances, be as descriptive as possible. Do any of them contain trauma?

I believe....

Sr. No.	Beliefs
1.	Others are to blame for my troubles, and I have been injured. _____
2.	I am unable to execute certain jobs due to physical or psychological limits. _____
3.	That what I do has no impact on others. _____
4.	I believe I cannot or will not put myself in the shoes of others. _____
5.	They would not suffer physical or emotional harm as a result of my actions. _____
6.	I believe I am hesitant to accomplish something that irritates me. _____
7.	I don't have extra money, time, or resources when others ask me to do something. _____
8.	To avoid things, I frequently develop aches and pains. _____
9.	I frequently feel exhausted, especially when I am not excited about doing things. _____
10.	It is permissible for me to ignore my responsibilities by either saying "I forgot" or completely disregarding them. _____
11.	I regularly expect others to do what I want, even if they do not understand why. _____
12.	I'm constantly expected to win, and failing is not an option. _____
13.	I feel it is legal for me to use other people's stuff as if they were mine and to borrow items without asking permission. _____
14.	My "wants" are actually "rights." _____
15.	Others regularly breach my trust and hence cannot be trusted. _____

16. Things will occur because I believe they will. _____

17. I can make decisions without first gathering information. _____

18. Despite evidence to the contrary, I maintain that I am correct and that my perspective is correct. _____

19. I believe that I should cling to my original point of view, even if it is proven to be inaccurate. _____

20. Thinking or preparing ahead is either unneeded or ineffective. _____

21. Fear is a weakness, so even when I feel terrified, I deny it. _____

22. I have discovered that employing anger expressions such as direct threats, intimidation, sarcasm, or passive animosity is an efficient approach to get what I want from others. _____

23. If things do not go as planned, I believe I will be chastised and found wanting. _____

24. I am powerful. _____

25. Others will let me down. I am confident that I will prevail in any conflict. _____

26. In and of itself, I appreciate a good debate. _____

Situations in which these beliefs determine actions:

_____
_____
_____
_____

Situations in which these beliefs govern my behaviour: Have you discovered anything new about yourself as a result of this exercise? Has it proven anything you already knew? What does it tell about the impact of traumatic events on you? (*If necessary, use your journal to write more.*)

_____
_____
_____
_____
_____
_____
_____

Activity 4: Ability to Cope with Trauma

Check those of the following statements that you believe apply to you.

1. I am highly extravagant (I enjoy being with people). _____
2. I appreciate the process of creating new experiences. _____
3. I am a pleasant person to be around. _____
4. I believe that my inner strength provides me with power. _____
5. I am confident in my abilities to deal with a variety of scenarios. _____
6. I try to break down complex problems into smaller, more manageable chunks. _____
7. I have a typically upbeat and optimistic attitude on life. _____
8. When possible, I take control of situations, or at least attempt to do so. _____
9. I am determined to overcome the negative experiences I have had throughout my life. _____
10. I have a reliable social support structure on which I can count. _____
11. My life conditions are crystal obvious to me. _____
12. I am a religious person. _____
13. I have a wonderful sense of humour. _____
14. I am enthusiastic about the future. _____
15. I am open to trying new things in life. _____
16. In certain situations, I can empathise with the emotions of others. _____
17. I am a proactive person who enjoys accomplishing daily duties. _____
18. I plan and structure my thoughts and activities. _____
19. I am driven to find solutions to the challenges that arise in my life. _____

What about yourself do you notice after reading these statements? Did you check all of these items?

_____
_____

Do you detect any patterns among those you checked or didn't?

_____
_____

The more you looked, the more likely you were to act and deal with the trauma you had experienced.

_____
_____

CHAPTER 2 POST-TRAUMATIC STRESS DISORDER (PTSD)

2.1 What is PTSD?

Post-traumatic stress disorder (PTSD) is a typical reaction to a traumatic incident. A PTSD diagnosis necessitates exposure to an occurrence involving death, the threat of death, injury, or a threat to your or another person's physical safety. Such an occurrence is usually associated with profound fear, helplessness, or horror. Additionally, you may experience one or more of the following symptoms following the trauma: re-experiencing, avoidance, or persistent sensations of anxiety or being on edge.

2.2 Symptoms of PTSD

Re-experiencing

A traumatic event might be re-experienced in a variety of ways. People suffering from PTSD frequently have nightmares about the event, have terrible memories of the trauma, and have times when they believe the trauma is happening all over again. Furthermore, when reliving traumatic events, you may feel extremely emotionally or physically uncomfortable. *For example, your heart may begin to race, you may begin to cry uncontrollably, or you may become extremely worried.*

Avoidance

Recalling the traumatic event (or events) can be incredibly challenging, leading individuals to take extreme measures to avoid any reminders. This may involve a strong reluctance to discuss or even think about the trauma. Additionally, individuals may go to great lengths to steer clear of people or places that trigger memories of the incident. In some cases, the avoidance is so intense that crucial details of the event cannot be recollected.

As a result of this avoidance, individuals may also experience a disinterest in life and a sense of detachment from others. Emotional numbness, particularly towards positive emotions, is a common experience for many individuals with PTSD. It may feel as though one is unable to fully connect with the joys and pleasures of life. Furthermore, there may be a belief that planning for the future is futile, and that one's life will not be long enough to experience the wonderful things life has to offer.

Constant Anxiety or Nervousness

One of the PTSD symptoms is feeling excessively nervous, worried, or on edge most of the time. You may, for example, have trouble sleeping and concentrating. Many persons with PTSD report trouble controlling their anger or feeling impatient. You may also be "on guard" a lot of the time, constantly examining your surroundings for potential threats. You may be quickly startled or reactive to loud or sudden changes in your environment.

Hannah was at home when the hurricane struck. She got out of her house safely, but she has a lot of thoughts and nightmares about the hurricane and is constantly irritable, jumpy, and angry. She begins attending a PTSD-specific treatment group at her school. She inquires about PTSD with the group leader, a school social worker. Hannah is relieved to realise that so many individuals have experienced comparable reactions to stressful experiences that the reactions have a name (PTSD).

Activity 5: Identify Your Symptoms Related to Each Category

Complete this exercise to determine which trauma symptoms you experience.

Constant Anxiety or Nervousness

1. You frequently have trouble falling or staying asleep. _____Yes

2. You frequently experience great impatience or wrath. _____Yes

3. You are frequently apprehensive and frightened, searching your surroundings for threats. _____Yes

4. You are easily startled (for example, when you hear unusual noises or feel attacked). _____Yes

5. You try to avoid ideas, sensations, or discussions that remind you of the traumatic incident. _____Yes

Avoidance

1. You strive to avoid people, places, and situations that remind you of the terrible experience. ____Yes

2. Even if you try, you cannot recall essential details of the horrific incident. ____Yes

3. You are no longer interested in things you used to appreciate before the terrible occurrence. ____Yes

4. You don›t feel connected or close to other people. ____Yes

5. You have difficulty experiencing emotions and feelings (for example, you are emotionally numb). ____Yes

6. You rarely plan for the future (for example, you sometimes believe your future will be cut short). ____Yes

Re-experiencing

1. You have recurring and painful memories of the event (such as distressing memories, images, thoughts, and feelings). ____Yes

2. You have had disturbing dreams concerning the occurrence. ____Yes

3. There are instances when you feel or act as if the event is replaying itself (for example, having flashbacks or pictures that make you feel as if you are back in the situation; losing your sense of time). ____Yes

4. You are tremendously unhappy when something in your surroundings, or a thought or feeling in your thoughts, reminds you of the occurrence. ____Yes

5. Your body reacts when you are reminded of the trauma (for example, sweating, beating heart, light-headedness, unsettled stomach). ____Yes

Activity 6: Scoring Your PTSD Scale

Do you think you have post-traumatic stress disorder (PTSD), or has someone ever diagnosed you with it? The following activity can assist you in determining whether you are likely to develop PTSD.

To begin, identify each experience that you are using as a reference point for your PTSD. If you have more than one, make copies of these pages and do this exercise for each trauma separately. Next, ask yourself about each symptom and how much it bothered you in the last week and what is the severity level. Finally, in the provided space beside each symptom, rate the severity and intensity of it from 0 to 4 scale.

Intensity	Severity
Never = 0 Only once = 1 2 to 3 times = 2 4 to 6 times = 3 Daily = 4	Not all upsetting = 0 Not all distressing = 1 Somewhat distressing = 2 Extremely distressing = 3 Really upsetting = 4

Frequency	Severity	Symptoms
		Distressing pictures, memories, or thoughts about the incident.
		Nightmares about the event.
		The sensation that the event was reoccurring or that you were reliving it.
		Being unhappy because anything reminded you of the incident.
		Being physically agitated by recollections of the event (such as palpitations, increased heart rate, hyperventilation, vomiting, and disturb digestive system).
		Refraining from the arousal of trauma-related thoughts and sentiments.
		Avoiding activities or situations that remind you of the event.
		Difficulty to recollect key details of the event.

		Having trouble enjoying things.
		Feeling disconnected from other people.
		Inability to feel emotions such as sadness or love.
		Difficulties in imagining a long life and achieving your goals.
		Having difficulty falling or staying asleep.
		Irritation or outbursts of wrath are easily elicited.
		Having difficulty focusing or sustaining attention.
		A feeling of being continually on guard, easily distracted, or the necessity to be watchful.
		Being easily startled.

Add the totals from the frequency and severity columns. The higher your score, the more likely you are to suffer from PTSD.

Score: _____

Keep in mind that only an experienced therapist or doctor can diagnose you with PTSD. The correct diagnosis requires one or more intrusive symptoms (the first five questions), three or more move avoidance symptoms (the next seven questions), and two or more body arousal symptoms (the last five questions).

2.3 Traumatic Memory

Our minds are incredible storehouses of memories, each with its unique way of preserving our experiences. Think of it like having a collection of different memory boxes. We have the short-term memory box, where fleeting moments reside, like the phone number you quickly forget after **dialling** it. Then there's the long-term memory vault, where precious moments are securely stored for a lifetime.

But when it comes to traumatic events, something curious happens. These memories seem to find their home in a different kind of box called the implicit memory box. It's like a hidden treasure chest buried deep within our minds. This box is filled with associations, emotions, and automatic responses that we may not even be consciously aware of.

> **Imagine this:** *You're walking down the street, and you catch a whiff of a particular scent that instantly transports you back to that fateful moment. Your heart races, your palms sweat, and you feel a surge of emotions flooding over you. That scent has become a trigger, unlocking the implicit memory box, and bringing back vivid emotions tied to the traumatic event.*

This fascinating connection between triggers and memories is what makes PTSD a puzzle of its own. Sometimes, you're acutely aware of the links between these triggers and the trauma they represent. Other times, it's like searching for hidden clues in a complex maze. Understanding your PTSD symptoms and their triggers can be a challenging journey, but it's one that will ultimately help you unlock the secrets of your own mind.

So, as you embark on your healing path, remember that your mind is a remarkable landscape of memories, each with its own story to tell. By delving into the depths of your implicit memory box, you can gain a deeper understanding of how your experiences have shaped you and find new ways to navigate the triggers that lie along your path to recovery. Some memories are so painful or difficult to absorb that the brain does not store them in words; instead, they may be stored in pictures, complete with all the emotions that accompanied the experiences. According to Michelon,

"Pictures are more powerful than words in aiding memory retrieval".

Activity 7: Revisit Traumatic Memory

One important reason to try to remember what occurred to you is to minimise your dread of terrible experiences. Despite their threatening nature, traumatic memories are not intrinsically damaging. Confronting your traumatic memories in a safe context, such as writing about them, speaking about them aloud, sketching about them, or finding other ways to deal with them, assists you to process and work through your traumatic history. You can incorporate those events into your past by using memory processing.

Ignoring trauma memories can preserve them in your current life, along with the pain, worry, anger, despair, guilt, and self-blame they bring. You can have a deeper understanding of what occurred to you and may feel outraged about the violation if you remember and process these memories securely. Remembering in a safe environment might help you gain control over your experiences and the dread that comes with them.

It is preferable to concentrate on trauma memories in the past tense rather than the present tense. This workbook is designed to help you manage PTSD and its symptoms.

If you want to address intrusive memories but are unsure about their significance or accuracy, use the following questions to fill in the spaces.

1. Regardless of whether you dispute it, does your intuition or non-logical understanding suggest that what you recall is or was real?

_____

_____

_____

_____

_____

2. Does the memory reappear even after you try to forget it?

_____

_____

_____

_____

_____

3. Is the recollection consistent with your routines, worries, behaviours, symptoms, health issues, or life circumstances?

_____

_____

_____

_____

_____

4. Is some of the occurrence hazy, or is the event represented by images?

_____

_____

_____

_____

_____

5. Is your memory fragmented or broken up?

_____

_____

6. Is your memory fragmented or in bits and pieces?

7. Is there anything about the event that gives you comfort, understanding, or enhanced resilience?

8. Can you corroborate your memories with evidence from other sources, such as persons, newspaper articles, or medical reports?

9. Do you feel more or less distressed when you think about or share your memory?

Activity 8: A Look into Yourself

Before you examine the traumatic events that have affected you, you should consider who you are. Your self-image serves as a guidepost for who you want to be and what you want to do in your life. Traumatic events might take away your sense of self.

The following task is designed to help you assess the state of your fundamental self, your essential identity, and whether it is in good health, reasonably healthy, or poorly. To gain a sense of yourself, answer the following questions and complete the accompanying statements.

1. **What about myself makes me feel good about myself?**

_____

_____

2. **What facts characterise me?**

_____

_____

3. **I feel competent (or in command of):**

_____

_____

4. I am valuable because I can be emotionally (and possibly physically) close to:

_____

_____

5. My fundamental ideals, or the truths that guide my life:

_____

_____

6. I have a sense of importance in my life because: I perceive myself as a genuine, authentic person because:

_____

_____

7. I place the following unrealistic and improper demands on myself:

_____

_____

8. A seminar attendee once told Mary Beth, "'shoulds' are lies; don't should on me and I won't on you!" With those remarks in mind, make a list of a few "shoulds" that regulate your life and are rigid:

I should_____

I should_____

I should_____

_____

_____

9. How would you describe your core self now that you've completed this exercise?

_____

_____

2.4 Section Takeaway!

Many persons suffering from PTSD find it difficult to discuss their symptoms and diagnosis. You may feel ashamed, powerless, or alone when you think about your PTSD. However, it is critical to remember that a diagnosis is only a tool. Examining, recognising, and comprehending your symptoms will assist you in selecting exercises that will aid in your healing. The symptoms do not have to define you, nor do they have to dictate your life. People are resilient, as evidenced by several studies. Several factors influence healing from a traumatic event:

- *Experiencing one terrible incident rather than several.*
- *Having friends and family who support you.*
- *Seeking help from others who have experienced similar trauma.*
- *Developing a feeling of meaning and purpose in your life;*
- *Believing that you can face life's obstacles (a sense of mastery);*
- *Maintaining your routines and remaining involved in daily life; and*
- *Seeking counselling if you are experiencing overwhelming symptoms.*
- *Using coping skills that assist you in confronting, rather than avoiding, your concerns and symptoms.*

Some of these variables are unchangeable. You cannot, for example, choose whether you have encountered more than one traumatic event. However, there are also other aspects that you may control, such as your amount of social support and your attempts to confront your concerns.

PART TWO: TIME TO HEAL FROM PTSD

CHAPTER 3: EMOTIONAL REGULATION

3.1 Emotions in PTSD

PTSD (Post-Traumatic Stress Disorder) is a *mental health disease that can occur after experiencing or witnessing a terrible event.* While PTSD manifests differently in various people, the following are some frequent emotional experiences connected with the condition:

Fear: It is a typical emotional reaction to adversity. People suffering from PTSD may experience acute and persistent fear, which can show as nightmares, flashbacks, and avoidance of situations that cause them fear.

Anger: Another prevalent feeling connected with PTSD is anger. People suffering from PTSD may be furious with themselves, others, or the world around them as a result of the trauma they have endured. Outbursts, irritation, and even hostility can result from this fury.

Guilt: People suffering from PTSD may also feel guilty or ashamed about the terrible occurrence. They may blame themselves for what occurred or believe they might have avoided it.

Sadness: Another typical feeling connected with PTSD is sadness. People suffering from PTSD may feel unhappy, hopeless, or estranged from others. They may also lose interest in activities they once enjoyed.

Anxiety: Anxiety is a common PTSD symptom. People suffering from PTSD may feel continually on edge or fearful of another terrible occurrence. They may also endure panic episodes, hypervigilance, and sleeping difficulties.

Numbness: People suffering from PTSD may have feelings of emotional numbness or isolation from others. Even in settings that would ordinarily provoke those emotions, they may find it difficult to experience joy or enthusiasm.

Not everyone suffering from PTSD will experience all of these emotions, and others may experience extra ones that aren't listed here. It's also worth mentioning that PTSD is a complicated disorder with many various manifestations and treatment often consists of a combination of counselling and medication customised to the individual's needs.

Activity 9: Identify Different Emotions

Activity 10: Mapping Emotions in the Body

Draw where in your body you experience certain emotions. Use colours or artwork to express how you feel about these emotions:

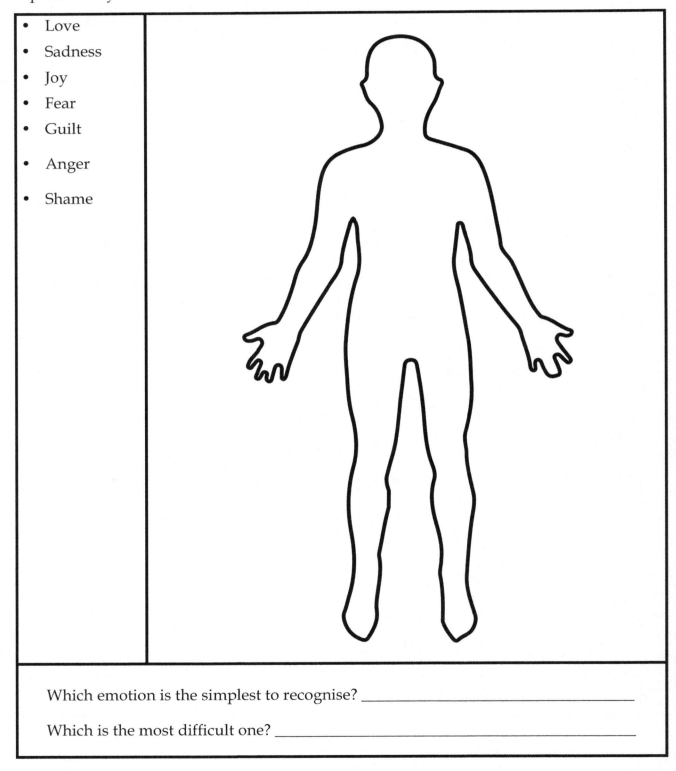

- Love
- Sadness
- Joy
- Fear
- Guilt

- Anger

- Shame

Which emotion is the simplest to recognise? _____

Which is the most difficult one? _____

Activity 11: Step Up and Take Charge (Relax and Meditate)

1. **Begin by taking a break**…Reduce the stimulus around you by going to a quieter location away from distressing stimuli.

2. **Stop what you're doing**…When you see warning indications of intense anger or unpleasant sensations and begin to think angry or unsettling thoughts, tell yourself to stop. This may allow you to relax and think more clearly.

3. **AIM TO RELAX.**

4. **Count to ten or one hundred.**

5. **Get yourself a glass of water.**

6. **Take a stroll (slow peaceful walk).**

7. **Take a few slow, deep breaths.**

8. **Return when you're ready**…Once you've regained control of your overwhelming emotions, return to the person or scenario that caused your emotional anguish.

Activity 12: Let's Take your Emotional Suffering Away

1. Pay Attention to your Emotions

- *Take note of its presence (without passing judgement on whether it is good or negative).*

- *Take a step back!*

- *Unstuck yourself.*

- *Remove yourself from your emotions.*

2. Feel Your Emotions

It's like a wave that comes and goes. Try not to suppress your emotions. Allow the emotion to flow through you. Avoid suppressing your emotions. Don't ignore the emotion. Don't strive to eliminate emotion. At the same time, don't try to suppress your emotions. Don't cling to it. Don't exaggerate it. Keep in mind that you are not your emotions. Don't always act out of emotion. Consider a time when you felt differently.

3. Experiment with Loving Your Emotions

Don't pass judgement on your feelings. Put your willingness to the test. Accept your emotions wholeheartedly. Respect your feelings. Don't presume it's unreasonable or based on false assumptions.

Activity 13: Increase Positive Emotions

1. Create Short-Term Positive Experiences

Do delightful things that are now possible. Do one thing from your own the *"Pleasant Events List" every day. For example, bathe in the tub, complete a crossword puzzle, play a card game, or write in a notebook...*

2. Create Beneficial Experiences in the Long Run

Make changes in your life to increase the frequency of happy events. Create a *"life worth living"* for yourself. Set goals for yourself. Make a list of the good things you desire to happen. Make a list of tiny steps towards your goals. Make the initial move. Take care of your relationships. Restore old friendships. Seek out new relationships. Concentrate on present relationships. Avoid avoiding...do not give up.

3. Keep Positive Experiences in Mind

Pay attention to the good things that happen. When your mind goes to the bad, refocus. Emphasise the positive and ignore the negative.

4. Let Go of Your Concerns

Distract yourself from thinking about when the good times will stop. Distract yourself from wondering if you deserve this pleasant experience. Distract yourself from considering how much more is needed of you today.

Fourteen questions to help you reminisce on what makes you feel better

1. My all-time favourite film is_____

2. My all-time favourite song is_____

3. Something I am very proud of is_____

4. My ideal day consists of_____

5. My most prized possession is_____

6. My favourite upbeat music is_____

7. I like to read_____

8. My ideal holiday_____

9. I don't do it often, but I enjoy it_____

10. If I could loosen up a little, I'd do it_____

11. If I wasn't so frugal with myself, I'd buy myself_____

12. My two heroes are_____

13. I feel pleased with myself because_____

14. I am thankful for_____

Activity 14: Emotional Regulation Worksheet

This activity will help you to identify which trigger is responsible for the arousal of a particular emotion and alteration in your behaviour. So after completing it, you can work onto handle that trigger. You need to write your trigger as a response arousal of a particular emotion. Draw your emotion on the blank face.

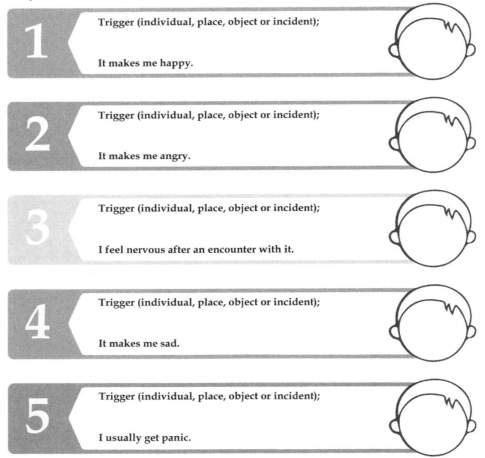

CHAPTER 4: VIVID FLASHBACKS

A flashback, according to Matsakis, *is a recall of a traumatic incident that appears suddenly and intensely, giving the impression that the past is happening in the present, along with overwhelming emotions.* An abreaction flashback can be a fleeting glance or a complete reliving of the unpleasant experience in real time.

4.1 Your Recurring Flashbacks

The occurrence of flashbacks is frequently unpredictable. Flashbacks generally refer to visual and/or auditory aspects of the trauma, but they can also refer to physical memories *(such as pain)*, emotions *(strong rage that appears out of nowhere)*, and behaviours *(behaving in certain ways when a trigger appears)*.

A flashback can give the feeling that the painful incident is happening again. It's important to remember that you don't lose consciousness, dissociate, or black out during a flashback. You may, however, briefly escape the current moment.

Flashbacks can recreate the intensity of your traumas to a great extent, and in some cases, it may be challenging to distinguish them from the present reality. This highlights the profound impact of trauma on you. Flashbacks can also occur in young toddlers, who might prefer to play them out rather than expressing them verbally. In some instances, children may act out what happened to them, such *as a nine-year-old boy performing a sexual act on a younger sibling, possibly during a flashback.* Making links between flashbacks can be challenging at times, especially when there are no specific events to use as reference points. Flashbacks might be explicit memories of entire scenes of awful events or just parts of them. A flashback usually involves an emotional and sensory aspect of the traumatic event. This means that when you have a flashback, your entire neurological system is activated; when you are exposed to trauma triggers, your neural system becomes hyper-aroused.

Flashbacks can occur as a result of a memory that you thought you had worked through. When this happens, you may find yourself wondering the following:

- *Can you figure out what the message or significance of the flashback is?*
- *Is the flashback attempting to convey any further information to you?*
- *Is there anything else you need to feel or experience in relation to this memory?*
- *Is there anything else you want to say or share about the memory?*
- *Is there anything else about your memories that you need to accept or accept?*
- *Can you hang on to this memory fragment without becoming overwhelmed or losing control?*

You can learn to deal with flashbacks in a variety of ways by using some of the techniques in this book.

Activity 15: Dealing with Your Flashbacks

Consider a flashback from the last two weeks.

Please offer a detailed description of the flashback you had and what you saw:

_____
_____
_____
_____
_____
_____
_____

Have you ever had a flashback like this before? If so, do you remember when it happened and under what conditions?

_____
_____
_____
_____

Can you explain any scents, tactile feelings, or sounds that you experienced during the flashback? Who was present in the flashback?

_____
_____
_____
_____

How did the sensory details of the previous traumatic incident compare to those of the flashback? Who was present during the horrific event?

_____
_____
_____
_____

What similarities and differences did the flashback and the horrific incident from the past share?

_____

_____

_____

_____

What techniques can you employ to make yourself feel better when a flashback occurs?

_____

_____

_____

_____

How can you stay grounded and focused on the present when you're having a flashback?

_____

_____

_____

_____

How did you feel when you finished this exercise? It is important to note that this exercise can be used to address any form of flashback.

_____

_____

_____

_____

Activity 16: Put it Out of Your Head

A four-step method for dealing with flashbacks. To utilise it, write down the answers in your journal:

1. *When have you felt this way before?*

2. *How does the current scenario compare to previous ones? Are there any similarities in terms of location, season, noises, or other factors? How are they similar to someone who was present through earlier traumatic situations if another person is involved?*

3. *How does the current situation vary from previous ones? What makes your current life situation, support systems, or environment unique? What sets the people around you apart from those who were involved in your previous horrific experiences?*

4. *What measures can you take to feel better now, especially if you feel threatened during your flashback? If your flashback is only an old memory that isn't dangerous, you may merely need to remind yourself that you can get through it, work through it, or try something new. However, if you are in danger, it is critical to recognise the true threat and take protective measures.*

Activity 17: Containment of Traumatic Memories

Containment is the process of diverting your focus away from upsetting memories, flashbacks, or thoughts by using your mind. It allows you to be present despite powerful emotions and helps you cope with traumatic recollections without reacting negatively. Practising containment techniques can help you handle intense emotions without causing harm to yourself or others. It is a deliberate decision that allows you to put up with upsetting memories until you are ready to process them. Containment, on the other hand, does not imply permanent avoidance or denial. Learning to hold memories reduces your need on numbing or dissociation to cope with tragedy.

Here are some strategies for dealing with traumatic intrusions like flashbacks, memory fragments, or ideas using containment:

- *Anticipate potentially stressful events and plan ahead of time.*

- *Allow yourself to cry to express your emotions.*

- *Write down your feelings and thoughts, or record them on audio or video.*

- *Distract yourself by engaging in repeated tasks such as puzzle solving or patience games.*

- *Remind yourself of your current surroundings to stay in the present moment (dual awareness).*

- *Put the memories in a container and close it mentally.*

- *To keep track of time, count to yourself or use a timer or pulse.*

- *Walking, exercising, or typing are all examples of physical activity.*

- *Use art to express yourself or to describe a memory.*

- *Wear a colour that you feel will make you invisible or allow you to blend in without being detected.*

- *Bring a camera to a potentially upsetting occasion and shoot images to avoid triggers by hiding behind the camera.*

Activity 18: Dunk it With Fun

The flashback prevention technique is based on the concept of dual awareness, which tries to merge the experiencing and observing selves and can effectively interrupt a traumatic flashback. To become proficient in this approach, it is recommended that you practise on "old" flashbacks that you have already processed and potentially resolved.

Apply this method in the event of a flashback including fresh memories or previously unknown painful content.

The flashback you want to narrate_____

You need to say it to yourself (noticeably) and fill in the blanks below:

Because I am recollecting _____,

I am currently experiencing _____ **and noticing bodily sensations of** _____,
in my body.

Simultaneously, I am examining my surroundings in _____
_____

specifically _____

where I can see _____,

thereby realising that _____ **is not happening now or in the future.**

How did it work for you? What are you feeling about it?

_____
_____
_____
_____
_____
_____

Activity 19: Flashbacks Worksheet

Fill in the table regarding your flashback. It will encourage you to move forward to get over your recurrent flashbacks.

1. Trigger before a flashback			
2. Part of trauma in flashback			
3. Thoughts and emotions			
4. Physical reactions			
5. Behavioural responses			
6. Coping methods adopted			
7. Duration of flashback			

CHAPTER 5 NIGHTMARES

5.1 Dreams Associated with Trauma: The Nightmares

You may have *dreams that repeat certain aspects of the trauma. These dreams may not necessarily cause fear, or they could be nightmares that wake you up feeling scared and anxious.* Dreams involving horrific occurrences might sometimes provide insight into what happened to you.

Activity 20: Define Your Nightmare

Because I will recall _____, I may have sentiments of _____ and bodily sensations of _____ during the night.

At the same time, I will examine my surroundings, realising that I am in _____, at _____, and noticing __ _____. This will allow me to recognise that _____ _____ is no longer taking place.

Activity 21: Recreate Your Nightmare

Fill in the blanks with a thorough account of your nightmare related to the trauma. If necessary, consult your notepad. Describe the scene as vividly as you can, including any emotions and sensory impressions such as odours, tactile sensations, noises, sights, and tastes that you recall. If you had several nightmares relating to the event, duplicate this activity and fill out a different form for each one.

_____
_____
_____
_____
_____
_____
_____
_____
_____
_____

- Is your nightmare a precise recreation of the painful event? Yes / No (Circle the correct answer.)

- Now consider how you could change the ending of the nightmare:

_____

_____

_____

_____

_____

_____

_____

_____

- What fresh knowledge does the nightmare provide you with that will help you understand what happened to you?

_____

_____

_____

_____

_____

_____

_____

_____

_____

_____

- How has your nightmare aided you in responding differently to your trauma?

_____

_____

_____

_____

_____

_____

_____

_____

Activity 22: Link Between Your Nightmare and Trauma

It is critical to analyse and attempt to comprehend the substance of your nightmares. If you are receiving treatment, it can help you analyse the severity of your nightmares and provide you with a safe space to explore any accompanying feelings. Nightmares can provide significant insights and may have both obvious and hidden significance. Addressing your dreams thoroughly may even help to reduce some of your hyperarousal and hypervigilance by accustoming you to their content and decreasing your avoidance efforts.

What are your reoccurring nightmares?

_____

_____

_____

_____

Do they appear to have content similar to the traumas you experienced?

_____

_____

_____

_____

Are unpleasant memories conveyed directly, in disguise, or concealed forms?

_____

_____

_____

_____

Is there anything that happens during the day that seems to trigger your nightmares?

_____

_____

_____

_____

Activity 23: Flower Diagram

- ✓ Write the nightmare you want to investigate in the centre of the diagram.

- ✓ Write down any sensory experiences that come to mind when you think about the dream in the first petal of the flower. Images, sounds, smells, and touch sensations are examples of sensory input.

- ✓ Proceed to the next petal and record your emotions and beliefs about the trauma. Consider the messages you received before, during, and after the trauma, as well as any inferences you have taken from the experience (e.g., feeling responsible for the occurrence, feeling frightened, etc.).

- ✓ In the fourth petal, write down how your body reacted throughout the traumatic event. Did you freeze, flee, cry, or become numb? Fill in the fifth petal with whatever emotions that come to mind.

- ✓ What did you want during your ordeal? Did you want to split up? Did you simply want to flee, or did you intend to assault the perpetrator? Fill in the sixth petal with your ideas.

- ✓ Finally, in the final petal, record any activities you participated in. Did you make the decision to disassociate and flee? How did you react to the situation? Did you participate in any way? If you can't remember certain aspects of your experience, you may be suffering from traumatic amnesia.

If you require more room, you can record the information on additional pages in your notebook.

PART THREE: IT'S YOUR TURN TO TAKE OVER

CHAPTER 6: TAKE BETTER CARE OF YOURSELF

6.1 Skills to Relax Yourself

Trauma can have a significant impact on a person's emotional and mental health. Relaxation skills can help reduce trauma symptoms including anxiety, hypervigilance, and flashbacks by encouraging calm and boosting emotions of safety.

Here are some relaxing techniques that can help with trauma recovery:

1. **Deep breathing:** *In this method, you need to deeply inhale by the nose to fill your lungs with air followed by a pause for a few seconds and then you exhale through your mouth to completely empty your lungs. This can help you to relieve anxiety by slowing your heart rate.*

2. **Breathing with Diaphragm** *entails inhalation into your belly rather than only in the chest area. Sit or lie down comfortably, put a hand over your chest and the other on your belly, and take a deep breath by your nose. When you inhale, your tummy should rise, and when you exhale, it should fall. Repeat for 4 – 5 minutes, concentrating on your breathing.*

3. **Box Breathing** *based on 43 strategies, inhale, hold and exhale for four seconds and then repeat for a few minutes, focusing on your breathing and counting.*

4. **4-7-8 Breathing technique** *entails 4 seconds inhalation, 7 seconds pause and 8 seconds exhalation. Repeat for a few minutes, focusing on your breathing and counting.*

5. **Breathing through different nostrils** *involves inhaling by one nostril and covering the other with the thumb, simultaneously holding breath and then releasing from the opposite one. For a few minutes, repeat this cycle, alternating nostrils.*

6. **Relaxing muscle progressively** *in this technique each muscle in the body first tensed and then relaxed. This can help you become more aware of your body while also encouraging feelings of relaxation.*

7. **Mindfulness meditation** *entails focusing on the present moment and observing your thoughts objectively. This can aid in the reduction of tension and anxiety.*

8. **Yoga:** *Practising yoga can help you become more aware of your body, promote calm, and decrease anxiety.*

9. **Visualisation:** *Picture a serene place, such as a beach or a forest, and concentrate on the details. This can aid in the creation of a sensation of calm and the promotion of emotions of relaxation.*

Activity 24: Relaxation Skills

Answer the following questions after doing each of these activities a few times a day for a few days.

What did you enjoy most about these skills?

_____

_____

_____

_____

_____

_____

_____

_____

What did you dislike about these?

_____

_____

_____

_____

_____

_____

_____

_____

In what scenarios might you employ this talent (for example, after going to bed to assist you in falling asleep? Before getting out of your car after arriving at school? or Before beginning a maths quiz that you are worried about)?

_____

_____

_____

_____

_____

_____

_____

Activity 25: Self-Help Coping Skills

Calming and grounding your body might help you control your trauma reactions. Calming and grounding abilities direct your attention to the present rather than what has occurred in the past. There are numerous methods for grounding and calming your body.

5-4-3-2-1

- *Describe five objects you perceive in the room.*
- *If feasible, give them specific names.*
- *Describe five sounds you can hear right now.*
- *Describe four items you can see.*
- *Describe four sounds you can hear.*
- *Describe three items you can see.*
- *Describe three sounds you can hear.*
- *Describe two items you can see.*
- *Describe two sounds you can hear.*
- *Describe one object you can see.*
- *Describe one item you can hear.*

Alternatively, you might try the following optional version.

Look for a room

- *Choose a colour and then name all of the items in the room that are that colour.*
- *There are numerous variations to this practice.*
- *Take a look at the image and list all of the colours you notice.*
- *You can name anything you see that begins with a specific letter.*
- *As you name each object in the room, you can count how many there are.*
- *The goal is to bring your entire, focused attention to your current location and let go of distractions from other places and times.*

Concentrating on grounding

- *Place your feet flat on the floor and sit in a comfortable chair.*
- *Take note of how you are related to the Earth.*
- *Feel the ground beneath your feet.*
- *Feel the back of your legs on the chair's bottom. Feel your back against the chair's back.*
- *Feel your arms on the chair's arms.*
- *Take note of how the chair provides support and connects you to the ground.*
- *Breathe. Continue to concentrate on how you are related to the Earth.*
- *When other thoughts enter your mind, gently bring them back to how you are connected to the ground.*
- *Continue to breathe and notice how you are connected to the earth until you feel more at ease.*

A physical examination

- *In your mind, slowly scan your entire body.*
- *Describe the sensations you are experiencing in each section of your body.*
- *Don't try to change the sensations; instead, observe how they change on their own.*
- *Try not to evaluate whether the sensations you are experiencing are positive or negative; simply notice what you are experiencing.*
- *However, keep in mind that this might be a tough skill for persons who have been sexually assaulted.*

For a few days, practise one of these abilities several times every day and answer the following questions:

What did you enjoy most about this skill?

_____
_____
_____
_____
_____
_____

What did you dislike about this ability?

_____
_____
_____
_____
_____
_____

In what scenarios might you put this expertise to use?

_____
_____
_____
_____
_____
_____

How did you use this ability without anyone noticing?

_____
_____
_____
_____
_____
_____

6.2 Social Support Groups

A support system is one of the most critical things you will need to recuperate from your trauma. In reality, a person's support system often predicts how fast and successfully he will recover from trauma. Your support system can include family, friends, and even people you haven't met yet. Creating and utilising a support system will be a crucial part of your healing process.

Charlotte's uncle sexually molested her. Her family is supportive, yet she dislikes discussing her ideas and feelings with them. She frequently believes she must be strange because she doesn't know any other girl who has been sexually molested. She even misses her uncle and the specific gifts and activities he provided to keep her from discussing the abuse. Charlotte soon began seeing a therapist who also leads a group for other girls who have been sexually abused. Although Charlotte doesn't know the other girls well or have much in common with them, it's wonderful for her to have a location where she can go once a week to talk about the sexual assault with people who truly understand what she has been through. By attending the meeting, Charlotte discovers that her emotions are common and that the majority of the other members of the group have had similar experiences.

Sofia and two of her pals are walking to school when they were hit by a drunk driver's automobile. Sofia and the other two girls were not close friends before the incident, but they became quite close as a result of it. They began to spend a lot of time together and help each other through difficult times. Even years after the crash, when they no longer spend as much time together, they rely on one another when they need to, even in the middle of the night. Sofia's recovery from the crash is aided by her friends' support and her ability to support them.

Activity 26: Good Social Support Groups

Kindly fill in the given space for the members of your social support group.

Family Members	Friends	Others

You are supposed to pick six in total people from your support group (preferably select two from each of the above categories). Fill details in the following section:

Person 1: _____

What the person did: _____

Person 2: _____

What the person did: _____

Person 3: _____

What the person did: _____

Person 4: _____

What the person did: _____

Person 5: _____

What the person did: _____

Person 6: _____

What the person did: _____

What if you notice that you don't have a large number of people in your support system? This is not unusual, but it is critical that you begin to establish a support structure for yourself. Who do you want to be a part of?

_____

_____

_____

_____

What can you do to include that person or those people in your support network?

_____

_____

_____

_____

Activity 27: Soothe Your Five Senses

Trauma causes tension and anxiety in our minds and bodies. It's critical to have things that you enjoy doing to help relieve stress and anxiety. Using each of your five senses to do something you enjoy will help you manage your tension and anxiety more successfully.

The activities listed below involve each of your five senses. Mark the ones you already do and enjoy. These are some things that may help you manage your stress and anxiety. Mark the activities that you believe you'd want to attempt but aren't presently doing to manage your stress and anxiety. Fill up the blanks with things you already do or would like to try.

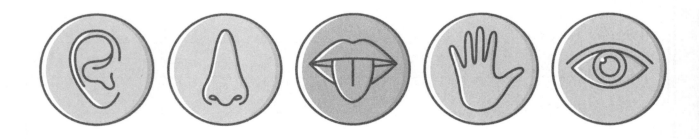

Vision Actions

- *Observing a sunset*
- *Enjoying a favourite book*
- *Seeing a humorous movie*
- *Looking at a favorite photograph*
- *Television viewing*
- *Magazine reading*

Hearing Exercises

- *Listening to music and watching waves*
- *Listening to children play*
- *Listening to birds chirp*
- *Listen to fan movement*
- *Listen to the morning breeze*

Taste Exercising Activities

- *Drinking a soothing tea*
- *Spearmint gum chewing*
- *Consuming chocolate*
- *Consuming a favorite food*
- *Cleaning your teeth*
- *Taking a bite of ripe fruit*

Smell-related Activities

- *A flower's fragrance*
- *A perfumed candle is lit.*
- *The aroma of freshly cut grass*

- *Petting a cat or dog*

- *Taking a hot bath*

- *Taking a seat in the sun*

- *Putting on a favourite shirt*

- *Using a stress ball*

Activities that use more than one sense are especially better. Consider doing something that will engage more than one of your senses. For instance, going for a run while listening to violent music and observing what you see and smell along the way.

Activity 28: Connect Your Thoughts With Feelings and Actions

Thoughts, thoughts, and behaviours are all interconnected and can influence one another. Most people read books like this because they wish to change their feelings. Feelings are difficult to modify directly, yet changing our thoughts or actions can influence how we feel.

Jill is nervous about returning to school after being tormented and beaten up. She resolves to shift her ideas to change her feelings, so she reminds herself that the bullies have been ejected and that her friends have devised a plan to keep her company between classes. Jill feels less anxious now that she knows this.

After becoming paralysed in a vehicle accident, Mia is depressed and sad. When she is depressed, she spends time on the web conversing with her pals, which helps to lift her spirits.

- Make a list of situations in which you frequently have strong feelings that you desire to change. This scenario may or may not be related to the trauma you suffered. When I walk up to my friends, they stop talking.

_____

_____

_____

- Write down the thoughts that come to you, as well as the assumptions and interpretations you make about those thoughts. For instance, they must be discussing me. They must despise me. Something must be wrong with me.

_____

_____

_____

- Make a note of an alternative perspective of what happened. For example, perhaps they had just concluded whatever they were talking about when I stepped up.

_____

_____

_____

- How might that affect your emotions?

_____

_____

_____

- Instead of adjusting what you're thinking, think about how you can modify what you're doing to affect your feelings. (For instance, I could go talk to another friend).

_____

_____

_____

CHAPTER 7: ARE YOU WILLING TO WORK ON YOUR STORY?

It is important for you to be able to convey your entire narrative concerning the trauma you suffered. Many people prefer to write their stories on paper rather than on a computer. These methods are excellent, but there are others. You may decide that painting, drawing, poetry, filmmaking, or even dancing is the best method to communicate your tale. The instructions provided here are for writing the story on paper, but you can write it in any form that makes sense to you.

Activity 29: Write Your Own Story

It is now your turn to tell your story. Write your narrative in as much detail as possible. You can always add chunks later. It may take several sessions to get your entire tale down on paper.

- Remember that it's crucial for you to be calm and relaxed when writing, so if the memories start to disturb you, if you start to feel fearful, or if you simply feel like you need a break, take a break and come back to it later.

When you've concluded a writing session, make sure to put the story away, both physically and symbolically. You could wish to use some of your talents to particularly stop thinking about the trauma and start thinking about something else.

Your Story

Activity 30: Add Details to Your Story

Your tale must contain a lot of particular information for it to be the most successful in helping you heal from your trauma. Including specifics about what you experienced, thought, and felt during the traumatic occurrence will help you work past the trauma as much as possible so that it does not haunt you in the future.

Return to your story and fill in the blanks. See if there is anything else you can add after each sentence you've previously written. You can add details in any order you like, but make sure you have all of them before moving on. It may take you some time to include all of the details. As you finish each task on the list, cross it off.

- *What did you see then, everyone?*
- *So, what did you hear?*
- *What did you smell at the time?*
- *What did you taste at the time?*
- *What did you then touch?*
- *How did your body feel at the time?*
- *What were you thinking at the time?*

Remain calm and relaxed when writing, so if the memories begin to distress you, if you begin to feel terrified, or if you simply feel the need for a break, stop and return to it later.

Remember that you have complete control over who sees your tale. It is critical that you include key elements in your story, even if they are things you would never want another person to see. Avoiding these details now may cause you problems later. Reread your story and add any details you may have missed. It's all right if you have to add these nuances in baby steps as you have with other things you were avoiding.

Your Detailed Story

Activity 31: Identify Post-Trauma Changes

We are altered by traumatic situations and the healing that occurs as a result of them. Some, but not all, of these changes are undesirable. True learning and growth can sometimes emerge from the most difficult situations.

Check off each of the following changes in yourself that you have seen as a result of the trauma:

- Difficulty trusting others.

- Avoiding persons who serve as a reminder.

- Interested in new experiences.

- I'm no longer interested in topics I used to care about.

- Avoiding places that serve as a reminder.

- More self-assured and aware of my surroundings.

- Less assured I'm closer to my family and friends now.

- I met some new folks.

- Understand who my true pals are.

List some of the additional changes that have occurred as a result of your trauma:

_____

_____

_____

_____

_____

_____

_____

_____

_____

_____

_____

_____

If you spotted any changes in the previous list that you don't want to keep in your life, identify them and devise a plan to fix them. For example, if you have trouble trusting people you don't know, you may try to chat with one person you don't know once a week to learn to trust your judgement again.

Changes you don't want to make and your plan of action:

_____

_____

_____

_____

_____

_____

_____

_____

_____

_____

_____

_____

_____

_____

_____

_____

_____

_____

_____

_____

_____

_____

_____

_____

_____

_____

_____

Activity 32: Your Real-Self

You are not the same person you were before the event occurred. In many ways, you are also the same person you were before the trauma. Whether or not they suffer trauma, most people change a lot during their adolescence. When you have finished healing from a trauma, it is a wonderful moment to examine who you truly are.

Fill in the blanks with the date and your answers to the following questions. You may want to repeat this exercise from time to time to see how things have changed.

_____

Five adjectives that characterise you best:

_____

The people who matter the most to you are:

_____

How you choose to spend your time:

_____

Things you despise the most:

_____

Your advantages:

_____

Your flaws are as follows:

_____

Where you hope to be in a year:

_____

In five years, you want to be:

_____

In 10 years, you want to be:

_____

Many people are afraid to show certain aspects of themselves. What are the aspects of yourself that you are scared to show?

_____

_____

_____

_____

How can you begin to show these wonderful aspects of yourself to others?

_____

_____

_____

_____

If you're not proud of these aspects of yourself, how do you turn them around and start showing them to others? For example, if you are opinionated, may you write letters to the editor of your school paper or join the debate team to express yourself in ways that are unlikely to hurt others?

_____

_____

_____

_____

Activity 33: Finish Your Story

The trauma you went through is simply a small part of who you are and what you will go through as a person. It was a significant part of your life for a time, but there is much more to your life.

Complete your narrative. You might use the story you wrote about the trauma you suffered, or you can just write about healing and the future.

You can complete your story using anything other than writing, such as art or music. Whatever manner you determine is best for you is OK.

Decide whom you want to tell your story to and then tell them. It's just as vital for you to share your recovery with people as it was for you to share your pain with them. *Congratulations! You have finished reading this book. If you need to return to the activities later, just get them copied/printed.*

CONCLUSION

In this transformative journey through the pages of the *PTSD Workbook for Teen Girls*, you've embarked on a powerful quest of self-discovery, resilience, and healing. Together, we've explored the depths of trauma, faced the shadows of fear and pain, and illuminated the path towards reclaiming your strength and finding inner peace. Throughout this workbook, you've delved into the complexities of your mind, unravelling the intricate web of emotions and memories that have shaped your experience. You've learned to navigate the storms of anxiety and nightmares, finding solace in grounding techniques and coping strategies tailored specifically for you.

But this journey is not just about surviving. It's about thriving.

You've discovered the power of your voice, bravely expressing your emotions and seeking support from trusted allies. You've explored the remarkable resilience that resides within you, transforming the wounds of the past into stepping stones towards a brighter future. As you turn the final pages of this workbook, remember that you are not defined by your trauma. You are a resilient, courageous, and extraordinary individual capable of reclaiming your life and crafting a future filled with joy, love, and purpose. Keep nurturing the flame of self-care and self-compassion, for it is through these acts of kindness towards yourself that you will continue to heal and grow. Embrace the journey ahead, knowing that you have the tools, the strength, and the unwavering support of your own inner warrior.

You are not alone on this path. Countless other teen girls have faced similar challenges and found their way to healing and transformation. Their stories intertwine with yours, creating a tapestry of resilience, hope, and empowerment. As you step into the world with renewed courage and a deeper understanding of yourself, remember that your story is not limited to the pages of this workbook. It is an ever-unfolding narrative, filled with endless possibilities and the power to inspire others.

May the lessons learned within these pages guide you towards a future filled with joy, purpose, and the boundless potential that resides within you. You are a testament to the strength of the human spirit, and your journey is a beacon of hope for all those who walk a similar path. Embrace the power within you, and let your illuminate the way for others as they find their own path to healing and resilience.

This is not the end but the beginning of a new chapter in your life—a chapter filled with strength, growth, and the limitless possibilities that await you. Remember, you are a survivor. You are a warrior. You are capable of creating a life that surpasses your wildest dreams. With every step you take, may you continue to rise, flourish, and inspire others with your unwavering spirit.

Your journey towards healing has just begun!

Printed in Great Britain
by Amazon

37614181R00046